HEINEMANN STATE STUDIES

Uniquely
Hawaii

Geok Yian Goh

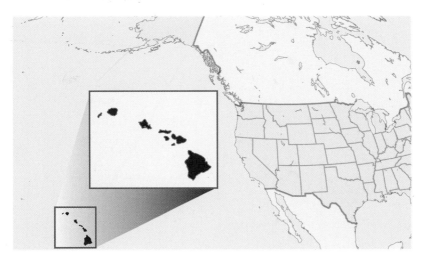

Heinemann Library
Chicago, Illinois

Designed by Heinemann Library
Printed in China by WKT Company Limited.

08 07 06 05 04
10 9 8 7 6 5 4 3 2 1

**Library of Congress
Cataloging-in-Publication Data**

Goh, Geok Yian.
   Uniquely Hawaii / Geok Yian Goh.
      p. cm. -- (Heinemann state studies)
Includes index.
ISBN 1-4034-4645-8 (lib. bdg.) --
ISBN 1-4034-4714-4 (pbk.)
1. Hawaii -- Juvenile literature. I. Title. II. Series.
DU623.25.G64 2004
996.9--dc22

                              2004002775

Acknowledgments
Development and photo research by
BOOK BUILDERS LLC

The author and publishers are grateful to the following for permission to reproduce copyrighted material:

Cover photographs by (top, L-R): Rick Doyle/ Corbis; Buddy Mays/Corbis; Joe Sohm/Alamy; Mark E. Gibson; (main): Corbis

Title page (L-R): Hawaii Visitors and Convention Bureau; Hawaii Visitors and Convention Bureau; Alamy; Contents page: Hawaii Visitors and Convention Bureau; p. 5, 18, 20T, 37, 38 Allan Seiden; p. 6 Corbis; p. 8, 17, 25, 28, 36T, 42 Douglas Peebles; p. 9, 40, 45 maps by IMA for BOOK BUILDERS LLC; p. 10, 20B, 43, 44T, 44M Alamy; p. 11, 15T, 16T, 30, 31, 34, 39, 41 Hawaii Visitors and Convention Bureau; p. 13T Joe Sohm/Alamy; p. 13B One Mile Up; p. 15M, 21T, 32 Sri Maiava Rusden; p. 15B, 6B Alamy; p. 21B, 22 AP Wide World; p. 23 Hawaii Historical Society; p. 24 National Park Service; p. 25 Buddy Mays/Corbis; p. 29 Mark E. Gibson/Corbis; p. 33 R. Capozzelli/Heinemann Library; p. 35 Jay Metzger; p. 36T p. 36B Rick Doyle/Corbis

Special thanks to Kathleen Rowlands, Director of the Summer Literature Institute for The Hawai'i Writing Project, for her expert comments in the preparation of this book.

Every effort has been made to contact copyright holders of any material reproduced in this book. Any omissions will be rectified in subsequent printings if notice is given to the publisher.

Cover Pictures

Top (left to right) surfer, U.S.S. *Arizona* Memorial, Hawaii state flag, luau
Main Hawaiian rain forest

Some words are shown in bold, **like this.** You can find out what they mean by looking in the glossary.

Contents

Uniquely Hawaii

Unique means one of a kind. Hawaii, located in the Pacific Ocean thousands of miles west of the **continental** United States, is unique because it is the only island state and the only state in the **tropics.** Before statehood, Hawaii was a kingdom ruled by native kings and queens. With its colorful heritage, Hawaii, the last state to join the Union, has contributed greatly to the **diversity** of the United States.

ORIGIN OF THE STATE'S NAME

Historians do not know for sure the origin of the name "Hawaii." Some believe it is formed from the two Hawaiian words, *Hawa* and *i`i*. *Hawa* refers to the traditional home of the Polynesians, ancestors of the Hawaiians, and *i`i,* means small and raging. Therefore, the blended name suggests a new homeland, one that starts small but will grow. Other historians believe that the name Hawaii refers to Hawaii Loa, the legendary Polynesian fisher who discovered the Hawaiian Islands thousands of years ago.

MAJOR CITIES

Honolulu, the capital of Hawaii, is on the southern coast of the island of Oahu. Home to about 850,000 people, it is the eleventh-largest metropolitan area in the United States and the largest city in the tropics. Honolulu stretches from the suburbs of Hawaii Kai in eastern Oahu to the naval facility at Pearl Harbor to the west. Honolulu is so large that in includes the white sandy beaches of Waikiki and the lush valleys and mountain ranges of Manoa and Palolo.

Hilo, located on the eastern coast of the island of Hawaii, is the second-largest city with a population of more than 40,000.

Hilo is the wettest city in the United States, receiving 128 inches of rain every year. Hilo is the gateway to the Hawaiian Volcanoes Park. On a clear day, visitors can catch a glimpse of the often snow-capped peak of Mauna Kea, Hawaii's tallest volcano.

Kailua, located on the northeastern coast of Oahu, is the third-largest city in Hawaii, as well as its biggest beach town. More than 36,000 people live there. The Koolau Mountains and beaches border Kailua. During **World War II** (1939–1945), the U.S. government set up a navy base there, causing the town to grow rapidly. Today Kailua includes a variety of resorts, businesses, and single-family homes. On a daily basis Kailua catches **trade winds.** These steady winds attract windsurfers, who ride surfboards with sails. Some windsurfers consider Kailua to be the windsurfing capital of the world.

Hawaii's Geography and Climate

Hawaii, the nation's southernmost state, is also the world's longest island chain. The chain is composed of eight major islands and 124 uninhabited **islets** covering an area of 6,459 square miles.

From west to east, the major islands are Niihau, Kauai, Oahu, Molokai, Lanai, Kahoolawe, Maui, and Hawaii. The island of Hawaii often is referred to as the Big Island. Each island is different in some way. Niihau is privately owned by a small group of Hawaiians and is closed to the public. Kauai receives heavy rainfall and is nicknamed the Garden Island. Oahu is the state's most populous island and is home to the capital city of Honolulu. Molokai contains tropical rain forests and the world's highest sea cliffs. Lanai is a secluded island that

Hawaii's lush rain forests can receive more than 300 inches of rain each year.

has been used largely for pineapple **plantations.** Kahoolawe is uninhabited. During **World War II** (1939–1945), the United States used the island for military exercises, such as bombing practice. Maui, nicknamed the "Valley Isle," is the second-largest island in Hawaii and is home to Lahaina, a historic former whaling town.

Directions in Hawaii

Hawaiians do not use north, south, east, and west to refer to directions. Instead, they use the terms mauka, or mountain, and makai, or ocean. For example, visitors walking along Ala Moana Boulevard in central Oahu who ask for directions to the Honolulu Academy of Arts will be told that it is two blocks toward the mauka side. If the visitors are heading toward the Ala Moana Beach Park, they will need to walk two blocks toward the makai side.

LAND

Undersea volcanoes formed the Hawaiian Islands over a period of 70 million years. After a volcano erupts, the lava cools and creates solid land. The Hawaiian Islands are actually the tops of a chain of volcanic mountains that stick up through the water's surface. The islands are still forming today because two of the world's most active volcanoes are part of the island of Hawaii— Kilauea and Mauna Loa.

The island of Molokai has the world's highest sea cliff at 3,300 feet tall.

Mauna Kea

When measured from its base on the ocean floor, Mauna Kea, at 33,476 feet, is the world's tallest mountain. Mauna Kea is home to an observatory containing the world's largest telescope.

CLIMATE

Hawaii's climate does not have the extremes of cold winters and hot summers, as does much of the **continental** United States. Mild temperatures mark Hawaii's year-round climate. Although often humid, the cooling **trade winds** make living conditions comfortable.

Hawaii's winter stretches from late October to April, when the temperature averages 72°F. Summer is May through October, when the temperature in downtown Honolulu averages 78°F. Hurricanes and hailstorms seldom pass over Hawaii, but thunderstorms, tornadoes, and floods do occur. One of the worst natural disasters

Average Annual Precipitation
Hawaii

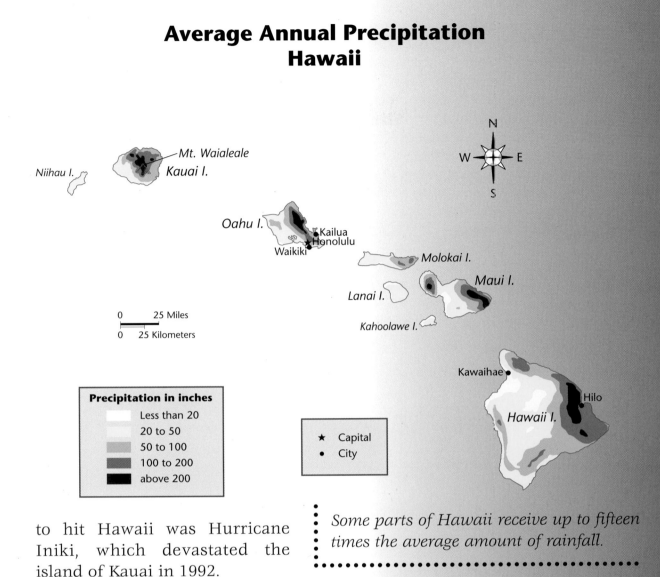

to hit Hawaii was Hurricane Iniki, which devastated the island of Kauai in 1992.

Some parts of Hawaii receive up to fifteen times the average amount of rainfall.

PRECIPITATION—RAIN

Rainfall varies throughout the state. On average, Hawaii receives about 25 to 30 inches of **precipitation** every year. Hawaii's heaviest rains fall during the winter. The **windward** side and the upper mountain valleys of the islands usually receive more rain than the **leeward** side. This is because the moisture carried by the trade winds often is blocked by the mountain ranges that divide the windward and leeward sides. The leeward side resembles desert landscape with its parched vegetation.

Famous Firsts

HISTORICAL FIRSTS

Hawaii is the only state that was once ruled by a **monarchy.** Native kings ruled the islands until the 1800s. Queen Liliuokalani was the first queen of Hawaii. Her reign ended in 1893, making her the last Hawaiian monarch.

In 1891, Hawaii's seventh king, King Kalakaua, became the first reigning monarch in the world to **circumnavigate** the globe. On this world tour he visited many countries in Asia and Europe, and he also went to Washington, D.C. Because of his trip, other countries established diplomatic relations with Hawaii.

Hawaii's Iolani Palace is the only royal residence in the United States. King Kalakaua

Known as the "Merrie Monarch," King Kalakaua threw numerous extravagant parties at the luxurious Iolani Palace, which is where Honolulu's civic center is now located.

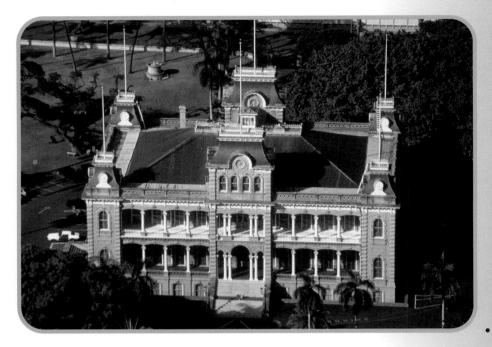

After renovations, Iolani Palace opened as a museum in 1978.

built the lavish palace, which was completed in 1882, at a cost of nearly $360,000.

LANGUAGE FIRSTS

Some Hawaiians speak a unique language that combines words from both Hawaiian and English. It is called pidgin or Hawaiian Creole English. There are twelve letters in the alphabet: five vowels (a, e, i, o, and u) and seven consonants (h, k, l, m, n, p, and w). The `okina (`) is sometimes considered a consonant. Most vowels are pronounced separately.

Official Languages

Hawaiian and English are the two official languages in Hawaii. Hawaiian is a Polynesian **dialect,** but it is considered to be a Native American language. In 1978, Hawaii became the first state to declare a Native American language an official state language.

ECOLOGY AND GEOGRAPHY FIRSTS

The Big Island of Hawaii is home to Kilauea, the world's longest-erupting volcano. Kilauea has been spewing lava almost nonstop since January 1983. The Big Island is also home to Mauna Loa, the world's largest active volcano. Mauna Loa takes up nearly half of the island's 4,038 square miles.

OTHER FIRSTS

Hawaii is the only state with its own time zone, Hawaiian Standard Time (HST), which is two hours behind Pacific Standard Time (PST) and five hours behind Eastern Standard Time (EST). Hawaii does not have daylight savings time. Because Hawaii is situated so close to the equator, there is very little difference in daylight from one season to the next.

Unlike other states, Hawaii does not have an ethnic majority, or a dominant group of people with the same ethnic background. Everyone in Hawaii can be considered a minority, or a small percentage of the population. Residents hail from around the world and represent Asian, Native American, and European cultures. People of Hawaiian or part-Hawaiian ancestry are the largest group at 22.1 percent of the population. Caucasians account for 20.5 percent, and Japanese Americans account for 18.3 percent of the population. Filipinos make up 12.3 percent and Chinese Americans account for 4.1 percent. The remaining population includes Koreans, Cambodians, Thais, and Vietnamese. Other Polynesians, such as the Samoans, Tongans, and Marshall Islanders, also live on the islands.

Hawaii's State Symbols

HAWAII STATE FLAG

Kamehameha I, also known as Kamehameha the Great, was king of Hawaii from 1810 to 1819. In 1816, he commissioned the creation of the Hawaiian flag. Its blue, red, and white design resembles Great Britain's flag because many of King Kamehameha's advisers were British. Its Hawaiian symbolism includes eight stripes that represent the eight major islands of Hawaii. The Hawaiian flag has lasted through Hawaii's transitions from kingdom to U.S. territory to U.S. state.

The puela *on the state flag is the symbol of Hawaiian* ali'i, *or royalty.*

HAWAII STATE SEAL

In the center of the Hawaiian state seal is a shield that includes eight stripes to represent the eight main islands and a star to sig-

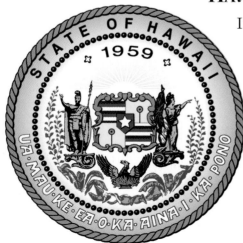

Adopted in 1959, the Hawaii state seal hangs at the mauka *and* makai *entrances to the state capitol.*

nify Hawaii as the 50th state. King Kamehameha I stands on one side of the shield and the goddess of Liberty stands on the other. Kamehameha holds a staff and the goddess holds the Hawaiian flag. A legendary bird called a **phoenix** is below the shield.

STATE MOTTO: *UA MAU KE EA O KA AINA I KA PONO*

Hawaii's motto, *Ua mau ke ea o ka aina i ka pono,* was officially adopted in 1959. It means "the life of the land is perpetuated in righteousness."

"Hawaii Ponoi"

Hawaii ponoi Nana i kou, moi

Kalani Alii, ke Alii.

Makua lani e Kamehameha e

Na kaua e pale Me ka ihe

Translation:

Hawaii's own true sons, be loyal to your chief

Your country's liege and lord, the Ali'i Father
   above us all, Kamehameha

Who guarded in the war with his ihe

STATE NICKNAME: THE ALOHA STATE

Hawaii's official state nickname is "the Aloha State." "Aloha" means many things, including *greetings, love, compassion, mercy,* and *pity* in Hawaiian. The word is a strong part of Hawaiian identity.

STATE SONG: "HAWAII PONOI"

"Hawaii Ponoi" means "Hawaii's Own." In 1874, King Kalakaua wrote the lyrics and Professor Henry Berger, leader of the Royal Hawaiian Band, wrote the music. King Kalakaua wrote the words to honor King Kamehameha I. The song served as the national anthem of the Hawaiian Kingdom from 1876 until 1893, when Hawaii was **annexed** by the United States.

STATE FLOWER: YELLOW HIBISCUS

The yellow hibiscus, called ma'ohauhele in Hawaiian, became Hawaii's official state flower on June 6, 1988.

Hibiscus flowers can grow to a height of six inches and have a texture similar to crepe paper.

When Hawaii became the 50th state in 1959, the red hibiscus, or the ilima, was recognized as the state flower. The ilima was a symbol of the Hawaiian monarchy. In 1988, the state **legislature** realized that using an old symbol of Hawaiian royalty for the Hawaiian state was unsuitable.

STATE TREE: KUKUI

The kukui, or candlenut tree, became Hawaii's state tree on May 1, 1959. Legend suggests that the Polynesians brought the candlenut to the islands between 300 and 750. The tree grows best in moist tropical areas, reaching up to 80 feet tall.

STATE FISH: REEF TRIGGERFISH

Adopted as Hawaii's state fish in 1985, the reef triggerfish, or humuhumunukunukuapua'a, lives in the shallow water off the Kona coast of the Big Island of Hawaii. According to Hawaiians, humuhumunukunukuapua'a means "fish which comes out of the water and sounds like a pig." The fish grows to between eight and nine inches long.

Native Hawaiians use the black dye from the nuts, bark, and roots of the kukui tree for tattooing.

The triggerfish is also called the pig-nosed triggerfish because it snorts like a pig when caught and taken out of the water.

Nene—Saving Them from Extinction

The nene was nearly hunted to **extinction** in the 1940s. Today, laws impose a penalty on people who kill a nene. The nene has changed over time to adapt to its rocky environment. Its feet are not fully webbed like most geese but are more like a claw, making it easier for the birds to walk over the hardened lava that covers parts of the islands.

STATE BIRD: NENE

Hawaii chose an official bird before it was a state. The nene, or Hawaiian goose, became Hawaii's official bird on May 7, 1957, while Hawaii was a U.S. territory. It reaches an average height of two feet. The bird is named for its call, which sounds like "nay-nay." Nene can be found on the islands of Hawaii, Maui, and Kanai.

Humpback whales can live about 80 years.

STATE MARINE MAMMAL: HUMPBACK WHALE

The humpback whale became the state marine mammal in 1979. The whales come to Hawaii around the beginning of November to mate and reproduce their young every year. They usually and stay until April. A humpback whale grows up to 50 feet long, roughly as long as a school bus. Humpback whales are usually black or gray, with white bellies.

STATE GEM: BLACK CORAL

The black coral, adopted as Hawaii's state gem in 1987, is commonly found in the deep reef slopes off the coasts of Hawaii. Coral is made of the skeletons of tiny marine animals. Early Hawaiians believed that black corals which would ward off evil. Today black coral is used in making jewelry.

Hawaii's History and People

The first people to migrate to Hawaii came in several waves from other Pacific islands. Some historians believe that this occurred between the years 500 and 750. These sailors reached the present-day Hawaiian Islands by crossing thousands of miles of ocean in canoes.

POLYNESIAN INHABITANTS

Polynesia is a group of islands in the central and southern Pacific Ocean. The earliest Hawaiian settlers were probably Polynesians from the Marquesas Islands and the island of Tahiti, both in the South Pacific. War or a natural disaster might have driven them from their original homes.

The Polynesian settlers on the Hawaiian Islands mixed traditions from their former cultures with new customs. Each island became an independent kingdom led by a group of royal chiefs called the **ali'i.**

Hawaiians are the descendants of Polynesians who paddled to the islands in canoes. They navigated by the sun and stars, wind and currents, and flight paths of birds.

THE BRITISH ARRIVE

In 1778, British captain James Cook was on a voyage to discover unknown lands when he came across Hawaii. Although the Spanish and the Portuguese claimed they had visited the Hawaiian Islands earlier, Cook is considered to be the first European to set foot on the Hawaiian

Captain James Cook first landed at Old Waimea in Kauai.

Islands. Although the islands were already named by the natives, Cook called them the Sandwich Islands after the Earl of Sandwich, an English-person who helped pay for his trip.

The inhabitants of the Big Island of Hawaii welcomed Captain Cook. Because Cook arrived during a festival honoring Lono, the Hawaiian god of agriculture, it is possible that the Hawaiians believed Cook was Lono himself. The two groups traded goods, then Cook's ships left. When Cook returned in 1779, fighting between his men and the natives broke out. The Hawaiians felt that it was wrong of Lono to return so soon. Hawaiian warriors killed Cook on the beach as he attempted to flee.

Russian Fort Elizabeth

Russian Fort Elizabeth lies in the Waimea Valley of the island of Kauai. This star-shaped stone structure is a **relic** dating back to 1816, when the chief of Kauai made a trade deal with a Russian company, who then began to build a fort. In 1817, before the fort was completed, Kamehameha, the king of all Hawaii, chased the Russians out of Kauai. The Hawaiians then finished building the fort. Today, Russian Fort Elizabeth is a registered National Historic Landmark and is the only Russian fort in Hawaii.

Each Hawaiian Island continued to be led by regional chiefs until King Kamehameha I used guns taken from a British ship to unite all the islands under his rule in 1810. With this bold act, Kamehameha founded the single kingdom of Hawaii.

AN INDEPENDENT KINGDOM

Throughout the 1800s, Hawaii was influenced by foreign ideas, particularly Christianity. In 1820, **missionaries** introduced the Christian religion to Hawaiians. King Kamehameha III, who reigned from 1825 to 1854, allowed missionaries to preach and to build schools, where they developed the Hawaiian alphabet and taught Hawaiian as a written language. Before this time, Hawaiian was only a spoken language.

In 1848, Kamehameha III passed a law allowing all people—not just the nobility—to own land in Hawaii. For the first time, foreigners could buy property in Hawaii, and many did. Some used the land to grow crops, such as sugar, that they could sell. Soon, American sugar planters owned more than 80 percent of all private land in Hawaii.

By the early 1890s, the powerful **plantation** owners in the sugar industry decided to overthrow the **monarchy** to increase their own power. With the help of U.S. marines from a nearby base, the plantation owners imprisoned Queen Liliuokalani in 1893 and created a temporary government.

AN AMERICAN TERRITORY

The plantation owners wanted the United States to annex Hawaii. President Grover Cleveland rejected this idea and tried to restore Queen Liliuokalani to the Hawaiian throne. Meanwhile, in 1894, the temporary government declared Hawaii a **republic** and appointed Sanford B.

On August 21, 1959, newspapers announced that Hawaii was the 50th state.

Dole as its president. President William McKinley, Cleveland's successor, favored annexation. In 1898, the United States annexed the islands and in 1900, Hawaii became a U.S. territory. Sanford Dole remained governor.

STATEHOOD

Statehood for Hawaii was first proposed in 1937, but the U.S. Congress rejected the request. One reason was that Hawaii was far from the U.S. mainland. Another reason was that Hawaii had many ethnic groups and Congress did not know if they all would feel loyalty to the United States. After several more unsuccessful attempts, Hawaii was finally admitted as the 50th state in 1959.

Queen Liliuokalani, a gifted musician and songwriter, wrote "Aloha Oe," or "Farewell to Thee," which is beloved by Hawaiians to this day.

FAMOUS PEOPLE

Kamehameha the Great (1740–1819), king. Kamehameha I, born on the Big Island of Hawaii, became the founder of a **dynasty** that ruled the Hawaiian Islands for more than 100 years. The name Kamehameha means "the one set apart." In 1810, he became the first Hawaiian leader to successfully unify all the islands under one ruler. Statues of the king stand in the Capitol in Washington, D.C., and in Honolulu.

Queen Liliuokalani (1838–1917), queen. The first reigning queen and the last monarch of Hawaii, Liliuokalani was a well-educated woman who believed Hawaiians should preserve their traditions and maintain independence, while at the same time adapt to the modern world. She became queen in 1891, but was overthrown in 1893.

Joseph Damien de Veuster (1840–1889), Catholic priest. Father Damien was born in Belgium. In 1864, he went to Hawaii as a **missionary** to introduce Christianity. Father Damien moved to the island of Molokai in 1873, a small part of which was then a colony for people with Hansen's Disease, or leprosy, a contagious disease that causes skin and nerves to waste away. In 1884, Father Damien discovered that he had contracted the disease, but continued to serve others until his death in 1889.

Hiram L. Fong (1906–   ), senator. Born in Honolulu, Hiram Fong was the first Asian American to serve in the U.S. Senate. He served in **World War II** (1939–1945) as an Air Force major. When Hawaii was admitted as a state in 1959, Fong was elected to the U.S. Senate. He built strong relationships with developing nations in Asia, including China.

Daniel K. Inouye (1924–   ), senator. Born in Honolulu, Inouye served in World War II with the U.S. Fifth Army. During the war, Inouye fought in both the Pacific and in Europe. He was injured while trying to take over a heavily defended hill in Italy. After the war, Inouye went into politics. When Hawaii became the 50th state in 1959, he became the state's first congressman and then later served in the Senate.

Father Damien's work to help people with Hansen's Disease on Molokai gave him a prominent place in Hawaiian history.

Daniel Inouye received the nation's highest award for military valor, a Medal of Honor, on June 21, 2000.

Patsy Mink was also the first Japanese American woman attorney in Hawaii.

Patsy Mink (1927–2000), congresswoman. Born in Maui, Patsy Mink became the first woman of color to serve in Congress. Beginning in 1965, she served twelve terms in the House of Representatives. Mink, a woman of intelligence and courage, was determined to remove all forms of discrimination and helped improve the living conditions of women, children, and the poor.

Don Ho (1930–), entertainer. Don Ho is Hawaii's most famous entertainer. Born in Honolulu, he claims Hawaiian, Chinese, Portuguese, German, and Dutch ancestry. Ho first began playing with his band in the clubs and hotels along Waikiki, Oahu. His music comprises mellow and catchy tunes such as his most famous song, "Tiny Bubbles."

Ellison Onizuka (1946–1986), astronaut. Born in Kona, Onizuka served as an Air Force test pilot for many years before becoming an astronaut. His first mission as an astronaut was on *Discovery,* the first shuttle mission flown exclusively for the Department of Defense. Onizuka was later selected to fly on *Challenger* on January 28, 1986. Just over a minute after it launched, the shuttle exploded, killing all on board instantly.

John Waihee (1946–), governor. Born in Honokaa, Waihee became Hawaii's first governor of Hawaiian ancestry in 1986. For the 1993 **centennial** commemorating the 1893 overthrow of Queen Liliuokalani, Waihee ordered that the Hawaiian flag be flown instead of the U.S. flag, thus showing respect for the Hawaiian monarchy that Americans had helped to overthrow.

Pearl Harbor

Pearl Harbor, located on the southern coast of Oahu, is one of the largest natural and **landlocked** harbors in the Pacific Ocean. In the 1700s European explorers learned that Hawaiians called it "Wai-Momi," or "Pearl Water," because pearl oysters were found there.

U.S. Naval Base

In 1887, the Hawaiian **monarchy** allowed the United States to build a station in Hawaii where U.S. ships could refuel and be repaired. Pearl Harbor was chosen as the site. Between 1908 and 1919, the U.S. Navy **dredged** the harbor to make it deeper so that larger ships could enter. After **World War I** (1914–1918) ended, the navy expanded the base.

December 7, 1941

On the morning of December 7, 1941, 33 Japanese warships and aircraft carriers gathered 230 miles off Oahu. The first wave of Japanese aircraft struck Pearl Harbor at about 6 A.M., surprising the

In the late 1800s the United States realized Hawaii was an important location for a naval base.

The Japanese attacks crippled a number of the U.S. defenses on the land and in the harbor.

American forces. The United States suffered 2,280 military and 68 civilian casualties, but a number of aircraft carriers and other military facilities survived the attack. As a result of the attack on Pearl Harbor, the United States declared war on Japan and entered **World War II** (1939–1945).

PEARL HARBOR TODAY

Today, Pearl Harbor is both a naval facility and a national historical landmark. The Pacific fleet continues to play a major role in U.S. military operations overseas. The submarines USS *Cheyenne* and USS *Columbia*, whose home base is Pearl Harbor, participated in the war against Iraq that began in 2003.

USS *Arizona*

Japanese warplanes sunk the battleship USS *Arizona* in nine minutes. More than 1,100 sailors lost their lives. Today, a 184-foot-long memorial commemorates those who died. Completed in 1962, it is directly over the sunken remains of the ship. It includes a shrine room and the ship's bell, which was recovered from the wreckage. The shrine room contains a stone plaque that lists the names of those who died. The USS *Arizona* Memorial, which receives about 1.5 million visitors a year, is the top visitor destination in Honolulu.

Hawaii's State Government

The capitol was completed in 1969 and renovated in the 1990s.

Honolulu, Hawaii's capital, is the home of Hawaii's government. The functions of the state are described in the state's **constitution,** or plan of government.

The Hawaii state constitution was created in 1950 and was called a state constitution even though Hawaii was still a territory. Amended when Hawaii became a state in 1959, the constitution upholds rights that are included in the U.S. Constitution, such as freedom of religion, speech, and the press. Like the federal government, Hawaii's state government is divided into three branches—legislative, executive, and judicial.

THE LEGISLATIVE BRANCH

The legislative branch makes the state's laws. It includes two houses—the Senate and the House of Representatives. The Senate's 25 members are elected from the 25 senatorial districts for 4-year terms. The House of Representatives consists of 51 members elected to serve 2-year terms. The head of the Senate is referred to as the president, while the head of the House of Representatives is called the speaker.

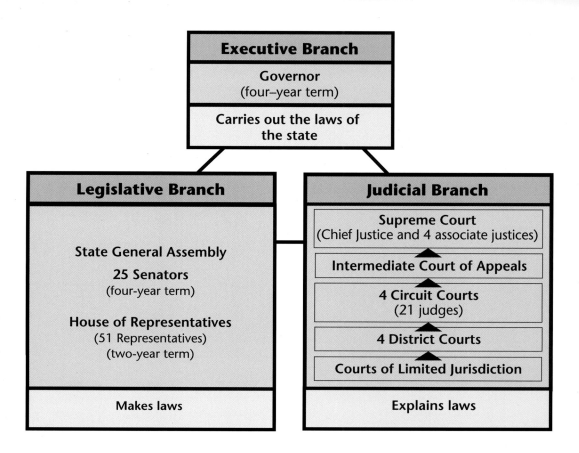

Executive Branch

Governor
(four–year term)

Carries out the laws of
the state

Legislative Branch

State General Assembly

25 Senators
(four-year term)

House of Representatives
(51 Representatives)
(two-year term)

Makes laws

Judicial Branch

Supreme Court
(Chief Justice and 4 associate justices)

Intermediate Court of Appeals

4 Circuit Courts
(21 judges)

4 District Courts

Courts of Limited Jurisdiction

Explains laws

A proposed law, or bill, must be approved by more than half of the members of both houses before it can be sent to the governor. If the governor approves it, the bill becomes law. If the governor vetoes, or rejects, the bill, it does not become law. The Senate and the House of Representatives can override, or cancel, a veto if two-thirds of the members of each house vote to do so.

THE EXECUTIVE BRANCH

The executive branch sees that the state's laws are enforced. The governor, who heads the executive branch, is the highest state official. The second-highest official is the lieutenant governor. This official assists the governor. Voters statewide elect these officials. They serve four-year terms of office and must belong to the same political party. A governor may serve no more than two terms in a row. The governor appoints other executive officials to head various departments of the executive branch. The state senate must approve these appointments.

THE JUDICIAL BRANCH

The main function of the judicial branch is to interpret Hawaii's laws and apply them to everyday situations. Hawaii has several levels of courts—the supreme court, the intermediate court of appeals, the circuit courts, the district courts, and other special courts.

The district courts are the lowest level of the judiciary system. They hear cases concerning minor offenses such as traffic violations and disputes between landlords and tenants.

Hawaii has four judicial circuits. The circuit courts handle trials, which include both criminal and civil cases. In a criminal case, the government accuses a person of breaking the law. In a civil case, a private citizen accuses someone else of breaking the law. The circuit courts hear appeals from the district courts. An appeal is a request for a higher court to reconsider a decision of a lower court. The governor appoints circuit court judges to ten-year terms. Judges may serve additional terms, but they must retire by age 70.

The intermediate court of appeals is the next highest court in the state. Like the district court, this court also hears appeals. It also checks court decisions for mistakes. The intermediate court will hear any appeal assigned to it by the chief justice.

The supreme court is the highest court in the state. It consists of the chief justice and four associate justices. The governor appoints the justices to ten-year terms with the approval of the senate. They may serve several terms, but they must retire by age 70. The supreme court has the final say in legal matters. The primary purpose of the supreme court is to review decisions of lower courts.

OFFICE OF HAWAIIAN AFFAIRS

The Office of Hawaiian Affairs (OHA) is a government agency and trust set up by the **legislature** in 1978. A trust is an organization that manages and distributes money to benefit others. The OHA's main goal is to protect the interests of the Hawaiian people and environment. It does this by giving funds for community events and by running events of its own. The OHA helps provide a better future for native Hawaiians and those of 50 percent or more Hawaiian ancestry.

About 80 percent of the state's population lives in Honolulu, the capital.

Hawaii's Culture

Hawaii's culture reflects the different influences of its many ethnic groups. It is a blend of native and foreign traditions from Polynesia, Asia, and Europe.

NATIVE HAWAIIAN TRADITIONS AND HOSPITALITY

Native Hawaiian traditions focus on hospitality and beauty. When foreigners arrived, however, Hawaiian culture suffered. Parts of the native ways of life disappeared, including the dominance of the Hawaiian language. In the late 1900s, Hawaiian culture experienced a revival and Hawaiians today are rediscovering their rich past. Some Hawaiian traditions that are popular include the **luau,** the **lei,** and the **hula.**

THE LUAU

The luau originates from the time of King Kamehameha II, who ruled from 1819 to 1824. The king held a great feast in which he ate with women, thus breaking a religious rule that required men and women to eat separately. The luau feast takes its name from the popular

Baby luaus often are thrown to celebrate a child's first birthday, where the decorations are imprinted with the baby's footprints.

dish of the same name. Luau chicken consists of chicken and the leaves of a tropical root called **taro** baked in coconut milk. Another dish is kalua, which is a pig roasted in an underground oven called an imu.

Traditional luau feasts were eaten on the floor and without utensils. Modern luaus often are held outdoors on grass or under tents. They often feature the same traditional food, but utensils are usually used. Typically, some kind of live music entertains luau guests.

THE LEI

The lei is a chain of fragrant flower blossoms, leaves, and other natural materials. Today, it is given to welcome or see off visitors, congratulate friends, and show love. It also symbolizes love, sympathy, thanks, and respect.

Since 1928, the first day of May is Lei Day in Hawaii. It is celebrated with lei-making contests, pageants, arts and crafts exhibitions, and Hawaiian music concerts.

According to Hawaiian legend, Hiiaka, a goddess of hula dancing and the sister of Pele, the goddess of fire, was the first person to give away a lei. Ancient Hawaiian chiefs were also presented with leis during their **coronation** ceremonies. Traditional leis are made by hand. Some leis are sewn with shells and others with bits of leaves and nuts. Each of the Hawaiian Islands has an official flower lei. For example, Oahu prefers the ilima, a small orange flower. People on Niihau string seashells to make leis.

Hawaii's Food

Like the diverse nature of Hawaii's population, Hawaii's food is a mix of native and Asian cuisines.

FOOD FROM THE TROPICS

Perhaps the best known example of Hawaiian food is a paste-like dish called poi, or cooked and pounded **taro.** Taro is the fourteenth most cultivated crop on earth. Another native food is laulau, which is chicken, fish, or pork steamed in ti leaves. Poke is cubed raw fish marinated with onions, seaweed, and roasted kukui nuts. Tropical desserts include haupia, a creamy coconut pudding, and kulolo, a steamed pudding of coconut, brown sugar, and taro.

Instead of rice and bread, the staple food of native Hawaiians is poi.

Asian Influences

Many popular dishes in Hawaii are influenced by Asian cuisine. These include the Filipino chicken adobo and the Chinese char siu, or roast pork loin.

Chicken Adobo

Adobo is not only the national dish of the Philippines but also a favorite with many people in Hawaii. **Have an adult help you.**

Ingredients:

3 pounds of chicken thighs cut into serving pieces

1/2 cup white vinegar

1/2 cup soy sauce

1/4 cup peppercorns, crushed

1 teaspoon brown sugar

3 bay leaves

5 garlic cloves, crushed

salt to taste

Combine all ingredients in a pan, cover, and allow to marinate for 1 to 3 hours. Bring the ingredients to a boil, then lower heat and simmer for 30 minutes. Take the cover off the pan and allow the mixture to simmer for an additional 15 minutes or until most of the liquid has evaporated. The chicken should be lightly brown. Serve the chicken with white rice.

Hawaii's Folklore and Legends

Folklore and legends are stories, sometimes based on true events, which help explain things or events. Hawaiian legends explain the origin of the islands, the nature of the gods and goddesses, and the origin of customs and rituals. These stories, an important part of Hawaiian traditions, are passed down from one generation to another.

MAUI LIFTING THE SKY

A long time ago, the sky rested on the earth. Plants and bushes were flattened. No matter how hard they pushed against the sky, they could only raise the sky a little. The sun had disappeared. The whole world was drenched in darkness.

A Hawaiian god named Maui, became very upset. He was determined to push the sky up over the treetops. He flexed his muscles and gave the sky a big shove. The sky now rested on the treetops, but the world was still in darkness.

"I will push the sky higher," exclaimed Maui, as he braced himself for the effort.

He pushed the sky and placed it atop the mountain peaks. However, the world was still dark.

"One more push," Maui remarked to himself as he gave the sky another mighty shove.

The sky finally came to rest in the spot where it is today. Soon the sun came and brought light and warmth to the land. The people cheered for they no longer lived in darkness.

KAUILA, THE MAGICAL TURTLE

Long ago, Honu-po`o-kea, a magical turtle, laid an egg at a place called Punalu`u on the Big Island of Hawaii. The egg was as dark and smooth as kauila wood. Afterward, Honu-po`o-kea and her mate Honu-`ea magically created a spring on the black sands, then swam out to sea.

The egg hatched to reveal another magical turtle. She was known as Kauila, named for the wood that her egg resembled. Kauila lived at the bottom of the spring that her parents built. Children played at the spring. Kauila sometimes transformed into a little girl to play with them, but she was also secretly protecting them.

"Punalu`u" means "diving spring." Legend claims that Hawaiians at Punalu`u were grateful for the magic turtle Kauila, who watched over their children and brought them a spring of pure water to drink.

Before the spring appeared, Hawaiians had to dive into the bay to collect fresh water from plants. Kauila's spring made it easier for them to get drinking water. Today, people visit the beaches of Punalu`u to look at the countless honu, or turtles, basking on the sands.

Hawaii's Sports Teams

Most people in Hawaii are huge sports fans. Hawaii's fans attend a variety of sports events ranging from baseball and football to surfing contests. Because the state does not have any professional sports teams, fans follow college and high school games.

COLLEGE SPORTS

The University of Hawaii at Manoa (UHM) features a variety of sports teams. The UHM women's volleyball team is called the Rainbow Wahines. Wahine means "woman." Since the establishment of the women's volleyball program more than 30 years ago, the Wahines have become one of the best collegiate volleyball teams nationwide.

The UHM Rainbow Wahines have been ranked among the top five women's volleyball teams in the nation.

The UHM baseball team, the Rainbows, or "Bows" for short, was established in 1971. The Bows have won the Western Athletic Conference title several times. In 1979, the team ranked first in the nation. They were also runner-up in the 1980 College World Series.

The University of Hawaii football team played its first game in the continental United States in 1923. In 1925, Coach Otto Klum led the football team to a 10-0 season. The football team was then called the "Fighting Deans," but now it is called the "Rainbow

Warriors." The 2002 team won ten games and went to the Hawaii Bowl.

SURFING

Surfing has its roots in early Hawaiian traditions. Riding the waves either lying down or standing on a hardwood surfboard had become an important part of Hawaiian culture by 1779. By the late 1900s, surfing had become a familiar activity at any beach where the waves are wild, growing into one of world's most popular water sports. In 1953, the first international professional surfing championship was held in Hawaii, and the state continues to host world championship surfing events.

Surfing was once called "the sport of kings," or "he`e nalu," which means "wave-sliding."

Hawaii's Businesses and Products

Agriculture and tourism are Hawaii's two most important economic activities. Another key industry is commercial fishing.

AGRICULTURE

Agriculture generates $2.9 billion for Hawaii's economy. Before tourism exploded, agriculture was the biggest part

Dole Pineapple Plantation

The Dole Pineapple Plantation is the world's largest producer of pineapples. In 1901, businessman James D. Dole planted his first pineapple tree on Oahu and founded the Hawaiian Pineapple Company. Dole knew that many people outside of Hawaii would like pineapples, so he created an efficient way to ship the pineapples out of Hawaii. He canned them. By 1950, it was the largest pineapple company in the world. Today, it is called the Dole Foods Company. The Dole Plantation is also a tourist stop, attracting nearly one million visitors each year. The plantation houses the world's largest maze, covering more than two acres with a path length of 1.7 miles. More than 11,000 plants, including Hawaii's state flower, the hibiscus, make up the maze.

of the state's economy. More than 5,500 farms in Hawaii provide 42,000 jobs. Pineapples and sugarcane are Hawaii's largest crops. In 2000, pineapples generated $101 million and sugarcane generated more than $63 million. Hawaii is the world leader in pineapple production

Hawaii is a world leader in the harvesting of orchids. It is a $20 million a year industry in the state. The state grows all the macadamia nuts produced in the United States and has the second-largest macadamia nut industry in the world, responsible for about 45 percent of the world's production. Macadamia nuts generate more than $38 million a year in Hawaii. Papayas are another of the top crops in Hawaii. More than 40 other crops are grown commercially in Hawaii. These crops include corn, soybeans, and sunflowers.

Hawaii is the only state in the nation to grow coffee. The state produces about 7.6 million pounds of coffee every year. Coffee is produced on the islands of Hawaii, Kauai, Maui, Molokai and Oahu. The first coffee industry was established in Kona on the Big Island.

Hawaii is the second-largest sugarcane-producing state. In 2002, sugarcane sales topped $64 million. The first sugarcane **plantation** was established in Koloa, Kauai, in 1835. Today, sugarcane is grown on about 70,000 acres on Maui and Kauai.

Commercial fishing boats use large nets that are dragged through the water to catch large amounts of fish.

Commercial fishing is also part of Hawaii's economy. The aku, or skipjack tuna, accounts for almost half of the fish caught off Hawaii's coasts. Fish sellers often label fish with its Hawaiian name instead of the name the same species of fish is called when caught in other oceans. For example, when caught in Hawaii, yellowfin tuna is called ahi. Sellers do this to make people feel the fish they are buying is fresher, because Hawaii has a worldwide reputation for fresh fish.

TOURISM

Air travel has been a boon for Hawaiian tourism. In the late 1950s, when greater numbers of people began to fly in commercial jets, it became easier to get to Hawaii. Today, tourism is Hawaii's most important business, generating $10 billion a year. About 6.5 million people visit Hawaii each year. A typical visitor spends an average of $169 per day in the islands. Visitors relax at luxurious beachside resorts, enjoy water sports, play golf, explore volcanic regions, and soak up the native culture. Studies have shown that tourists are increasingly interested in exotic vacations that involve **ecotourism** and adventure. Hawaii offers these types of vacations and is constantly adding more. Agtourism, or agricultural tourism, is becoming a popular choice for Hawaii's visitors. They tour farms or plantations to see how animals are raised and how food is grown and harvested.

*Halekulani in Oahu is a favorite spot for tourists. There are regular shows featuring **hula** dances and island music.*

Attractions and Landmarks

Tourists from around the world visit Hawaii each year. Each island has its own attractions, many of which showcase the state's natural beauty.

Places to see in Hawaii

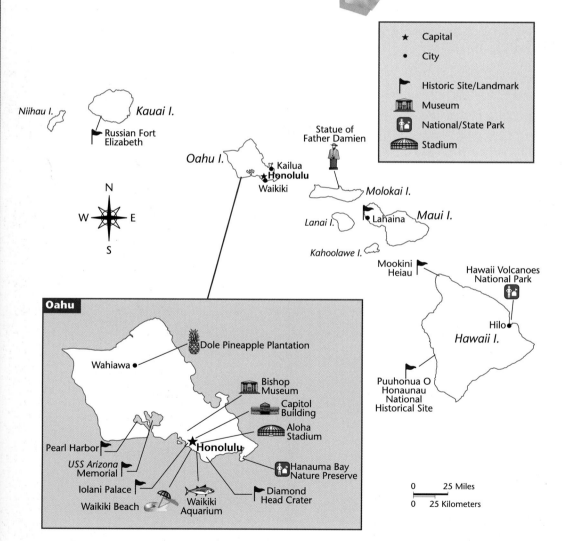

Legend:
- ★ Capital
- • City
- ⚑ Historic Site/Landmark
- 🏛 Museum
- 👥 National/State Park
- 🏛 Stadium

Niihau I.

Kauai I.
⚑ Russian Fort Elizabeth

Oahu I.

Statue of Father Damien

N
W E
S

★ Kailua
Honolulu
Waikiki

Molokai I.

Lanai I. • Lahaina Maui I.

Kahoolawe I.

Mookini Heiau ⚑

Hawaii Volcanoes National Park 👥

Hilo •

Hawaii I.

Puuhonua O Honaunau National Historical Site

Oahu

🍍 Dole Pineapple Plantation

Wahiawa •

🏛 Bishop Museum

Capitol Building

Aloha Stadium

Pearl Harbor ⚑

★ Honolulu

USS Arizona Memorial ⚑

👥 Hanauma Bay Nature Preserve

Iolani Palace ⚑

Waikiki Beach 🏖

🐟 Waikiki Aquarium

⚑ Diamond Head Crater

0 — 25 Miles
0 — 25 Kilometers

Kilauea's rivers of lava often flow down into the Pacific Ocean.

BIG ISLAND: HAWAII VOLCANOES NATIONAL PARK

Hawaii Volcanoes National Park has become one of Hawaii's leading tourist attractions since its founding in 1916. It stretches from the central to the southeastern part of the Big Island. It is home to the world's largest active volcano, Kilauea. Kilauea means "much spreading." In Hawaiian mythology, it is said to be the home of Pele, the goddess of fire. Kilauea has been erupting non-stop since 1983. These eruptions, however, do not appear as tremendous explosions, but rather as an always-bubbling pool of lava. Since 1983, lava rivers have destroyed sections of rainforests and hundreds of homes. The damage has cost more than $60 million. Yet as the lava cools it forms hard, black lava deserts. This adds acres of new land to the island.

Visitors can drive the 50 miles of road or hike through the park. Unique sites in the park include Halemaumau Crater, Thurston Lava Tube, and Chain of Craters Road. Halemaumau Crater, a part of Kilauea, is a pit of volcanic activity. The Thurston Lava Tube is a 450-foot tunnel that was formed when the outer shell of a lava river hardened while the molten interior continued to flow. Once the lava drained completely, it left a cave-like structure. The Chain of Craters Road is a 40-mile-long

Mookini Heiau, a very old temple, is dedicated to the ancient royal ceremonies of the Hawaiian monarchs.

road that runs to the ocean. Along it, visitors can see craters, hardened lava flows, and ancient rock carvings.

BIG ISLAND: MOOKINI HEIAU

Mookini **Heiau,** on the northern Kohala coast of the Big Island, is Hawaii's biggest, most ancient, and sacred site. It is a 1,500-year-old religious center, once used by Hawaiian kings to pray and offer **sacrifices.** At the site stands a massive three-story stone temple, built in A.D. 480. It was dedicated to Ku, the Hawaiian god of war. It is believed that 18,000 men were used to move the stones for constructing the temple.

BIG ISLAND: PUUHONUA O HONAUNAU NATIONAL HISTORICAL SITE

Puuhonua O Honaunau National Historical Site contains a 182-acre park, temple, and ruins. It was established as a park in 1961. However, as a sacred site, it dates back to sometime between the 1400s and the 1600s. In Hawaiian, "Puuhonua O Honaunau" means "place of refuge at Honaunau Bay." Until the early 1800s, Hawaiians went to Puuhonua O Honaunau to feel safe. Some went when they broke a law that they thought would anger the gods. A priest there would help them apologize for their mistake. Warriors who were defeated in battle also went there to avoid more fighting.

Hale o Keawe is a 21-foot-high temple on the grounds. It was built in 1650 and reconstructed in 1984 after time and termites had damaged the original building. The temple contains three **terraces** and an **amphitheater.** Ancient wooden statues called kii were placed at the temple to stand guard over the royalty buried inside. The temple, the park, and other features including a pond stocked with fish, several thatched house-like structures, and huge stones are all surrounded by a 10-foot-high stonewall.

OAHU: BISHOP MUSEUM

Located in Honolulu is the Bishop Museum, which houses the world's greatest collection of natural and cultural artifacts from Hawaii and the Pacific. The museum is a four-story lava-rock structure named after Charles Reed Bishop. Bishop, who was the husband of the Hawaiian princess Bernice Pauahi, established the museum in honor of his wife's last wishes. Some of the exhibits include the great-feathered capes of the Hawaiian kings and chiefs and the skeleton of a 50-foot-long whale.

Diamond Head Crater

Diamond Head Crater in Honolulu is one of Hawaii's most famous landmarks. The 760-foot-high volcanic crater formed about one-half million years ago. There was once a temple located on the western slope, and some Hawaiians consider it a sacred site. The name "Diamond Head" dates back to the 1800s, when British sailors picked up rocks that looked like diamonds.

The coral reefs circling Hawaii's islands can be damaged by and damaging to humans. Although they are fragile life forms that can be broken, coral can be sharp as knives.

OAHU: WAIKIKI AQUARIUM

The Waikiki Aquarium, located on Waikiki Beach on the southern coast of Oahu, is a historic aquatic museum that opened in 1904. It is built next to a live coral reef. The aquarium features sharks, eels, the endangered Hawaiian monk seal, and green sea turtles. One unusual exhibit is a spiral-shelled tropical mollusk called a nautilus. The nautilus is a relative of the octopus. Waikiki Aquarium was the first aquarium to display a living nautilus born in **captivity.**

Mark Twain, author of Tom Sawyer, *called Waimea Canyon "the Grand Canyon of the Pacific."*

MAUI—HALEAKALA NATIONAL PARK

Haleakala National Park, located in South Maui, is Maui's main attraction. Haleakala, which means "house of the sun," is a volcanic mountain that contains the world's largest **dormant** volcano crater. Haleakala rises 10,023 feet high. Its crater is about 20 miles around.

KAUAI—WAIMEA CANYON

Waimea Canyon, on the western coast of Kauai, is about ten miles long, more than one mile wide, and more than 3,500 feet deep. It is the largest canyon in the Pacific. This massive ravine is known for its reddish lava beds. Over approximately four million years, water and wind carved this enormous gorge.

Map of Hawaii

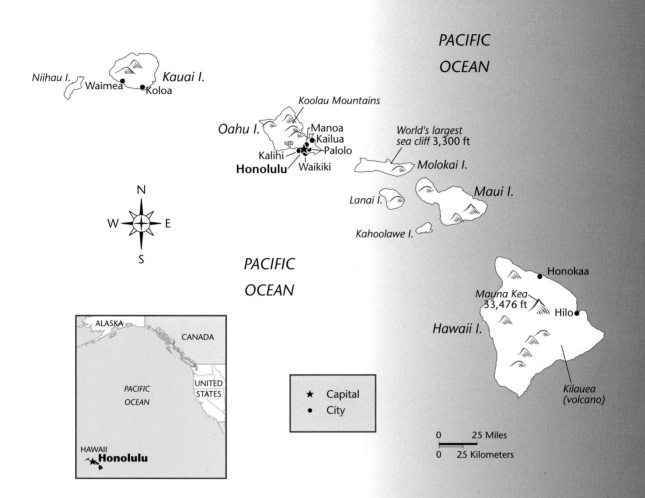

PACIFIC
OCEAN

Niihau I.   Waimea   Kauai I.
          Koloa

Koolau Mountains

Oahu I.   Manoa
      Kailua
   Kalihi   Palolo
Honolulu   Waikiki

World's largest
sea cliff 3,300 ft
     Molokai I.

Lanai I.   Maui I.

Kahoolawe I.

N
W   E
S

PACIFIC
OCEAN

Honokaa

Mauna Kea
33,476 ft
      Hilo

Hawaii I.

Kilauea
(volcano)

ALASKA
CANADA
PACIFIC
OCEAN
UNITED
STATES
HAWAII
Honolulu

★ Capital
● City

0   25 Miles
0   25 Kilometers

Glossary

ali'i   Hawaiian word for royalty or nobility

amphitheater   a large oval or circular stadium where events such as plays and contests take place

annex   to take over a territory and add it to another country

captivity   the state of being captured

centennial   a celebration of the 100th anniversary of something

circumnavigate   to travel around by ship or plane

constitution   a law describing the rules of a government

continental   refers to the mainland of the United States; of the 50 states, only Hawaii and Alaska are not part of the continental U.S.

coronation   the ceremony of installing a new monarch

dialect   a variation of a language that is spoken by people in a certain geographical region

diversity   the presence of a variety of different people or customs

dormant   something that is not active but that might become active again

dredge   to use machines to remove material from the bottom of a body of water

dynasty   a sequence of political leaders from the same family

ecotourism   pleasure travel in which people observe wildlife or help preserve nature

extinction   a state of no longer existing; in terms of volcanoes, extinction describes one that will no longer erupt

heiau   Hawaiian temple, or place of worship

hula   a traditional Polynesian dance

islet   a small island

landlocked   a section of land that is not touching any major bodies of water

leeward   the region of the islands where the dry habitat dominates

legislature   the branch of a government that makes laws

lei   a circular necklace of flowers that is a popular decoration in Hawaii

luau   a Hawaiian feast

missionary   a person who travels to other countries to introduce religion

phoenix   a legendary bird that could never die

plantation   a large estate where crops are grown, often in tropical climates

relic   an object from a long-ago time or culture

republic   a form of government which has no monarch and in which the citizens elect politicians to represent them

sacrifice   a ritual in which a person or animal is killed to please a god or goddess

taro   an edible tropical root

terrace   a flat paved surface on the outside of a house or structure where people can meet

trade winds   steady winds blowing from east to west near the equator

tropics   the region around the equator, characterized by a hot climate

windward   the region of the islands that is wetter and windier than the other regions

World War I   (1914–1918) a war in which countries including Great Britain, France, Russia, Belgium, Italy, Japan, and the United States defeated countries including Germany, Austria-Hungary, Turkey, and Bulgaria

World War II   (1939–1945) a war in which countries including Great Britain, France, the Soviet Union, and the United States defeated counties including Germany, Italy, and Japan

More Books to Read

• •

Knapp, Ron. *Hawaii (States)*. Berkeley Heights, NJ: Enslow, 2002.

McAuliffe, Emily. *Hawaii: Facts and Symbols*. Mankato, Minn.: Bridgestone Books, 2000.

Neri, P. J. *Hawaii (From Sea to Shining Sea, Second Series)*. New York: Children's Press, 2003.

Rice Jr., Earle. *The Bombing of Pearl Harbor (World History)*. San Diego: Lucent Books, 2000.

Sullivan, Jody. *Hawaii (Land of Liberty)*. Mankato, Minn.: Bridgestone Books, 2003.

Index

About the Authors

Geok Yian Goh is a writer and student who currently lives in Hawaii.

D.J. Ross is a writer and educator with more than 25 years of experience in education. He has lived in many states and frequently travels to other areas of the country. He lives in the Midwest with his three basset hounds.